THE RICHES OF THE WEST

A SOURCEBOOK ON THE AMERICAN WEST

THE RICHES
OF THE WEST

A SOURCEBOOK ON THE AMERICAN WEST

Edited by Carter Smith

AMERICAN ALBUMS FROM THE COLLECTIONS OF
THE LIBRARY OF CONGRESS

THE MILLBROOK PRESS, *Brookfield, Connecticut*

Cover: "Gold Mining in California." Lithograph by Currier & Ives, 1871.

Title Page: "Scattering the Riders." Painting by Charles M. Russell.

Contents Page: "The Independent Gold Hunter on his Way to California: I Neither Borrow nor Lend." Lithograph by Currier & Ives.

Back Cover: "Prize Fat Cattle." Lithograph by Currier & Ives.

Library of Congress Cataloging-in-Publication Data

The Riches of the West: a sourcebook on the American West / edited by Carter Smith.
      p. cm. -- (American albums from the collections of the Library of Congress)
    Includes bibliographical references and index.
    Summary: Uses contemporary pictures and maps in presenting the story of the trappers, miners, ranchers, and farmers who turned a huge wilderness into the "breadbasket of the world."
    ISBN 1-56294-132-1 (lib. bdg.) ISBN 0-7613-0155-0 (pbk.)
    1. West (U.S.)--Economic conditions--Juvenile literature 2. West (U.S.)--Economic conditions--Sources--Juvenile literature. 3. West (U.S.)--Industries--History--Juvenile literature. 4. West (U.S.)--Industries--History--Sources--Juvenile literature. 5. Frontier and pioneer life--West (U.S.)--Juvenile literature. 6. Frontier and pioneer life--West (U.S.)--Sources--Juvenile literature. [1. West (U.S.)--Industries--History. 2. Frontier and pioneer life--West (U.S.)] I. Smith, C. Carter. II. Series.
HC107.A17R53 1992
338.0978--dc20
                                            91-31127
                                                CIP
                                                  AC

Created in association with Media Projects Incorporated

C. Carter Smith, *Executive Editor*
Lelia Wardwell, *Managing Editor*
Elizabeth Prince, *Manuscript Editor*
Kevin Osborn, *Principal Writer*
Kimberly Horstman, *Researcher*
Lydia Link, *Designer*
Athena Angelos, *Photo Researcher*

The consultation of Bernard F. Reilly, Jr., Head Curator of the Prints and Photographs Division of the Library of Congress, is gratefully acknowledged.

10 9 8 7 6 5 4 3 2 1

Contents

"The Pioneer Cabin of the Yosemite" is a Currier & Ives print.

Introduction

THE RICHES OF THE WEST is one of the volumes in a series published by The Millbrook Press titled AMERICAN ALBUMS FROM THE COLLECTIONS OF THE LIBRARY OF CONGRESS and one of six books in the series subtitled SOURCEBOOKS ON THE AMERICAN WEST. They treat the history of the West from pioneer days to the early twentieth century.

The editors' goal for the series is to make available to the student many of the original visual documents of the American past that are preserved in the Library of Congress. Featured prominently in THE RICHES OF THE WEST are the rich holdings of early maps, prints, and original book and magazine illustrations preserved in the Library's Geography and Map Division, the Division of Prints and Photographs, and its general collections. These pictorial records today offer a wealth of insight into their times, both in what they show and in how they themselves came about.

Essential to the extraordinary expansion of American territory westward during the nineteenth century was the mapping of these regions. The federal government was forced by economic and political realities to take stock almost continually of its growing dominions. Borders were constantly changing and subject to legal and international dispute. There were persistent claims and designs on American territories by European powers. And new areas were constantly being opened by traders and settlers. The many federally-subsidized exploring expeditions, such as that of Lewis and Clark from 1804 to 1806, resulted in maps that permitted a measure of government control, and today nicely illustrate the nineteenth-century Americans' expanding knowledge of their frontier.

In the early nineteenth century, the exotic mythology of frontier life was created in drawings and paintings by artists such as Arthur Fitzwilliam Tait and F. O. C. Darley. Their portrayals of the lives and exploits of trappers and hunters emphasized the rare moments of danger and high adventure, in lives that were more often marked by hardship, brutality, and monotony. Similarly, after the Civil War, the illustrators of *Century* magazine, *Harper's*, and other journals chronicled the romantic aspects of cowboy life, the varying fortunes of prospectors, and the unruly and violent character of mining towns and camps. Enterprising editors from these journals sent artists to the West specifically in search of authenticity and color. The natural wonders of the region also fascinated Eastern readers, who never seemed to tire of images of men and women dwarfed by the colossal redwoods of California and the geological spectacles of Yellowstone.

The works reproduced here represent a small but telling portion of this rich record of Western life. These are preserved for us today by the Library of Congress in its role as the nation's library.

BERNARD F. REILLY, JR.

A TIMELINE OF MAJOR EVENTS
1763-1807

UNITED STATES HISTORY

1776 Twelve of the thirteen colonies send delegates to Philadelphia for the signing of the Declaration of Independence.

1783 The Revolutionary War ends when the U.S. and Britain sign the Treaty of Paris.

1787 Delegates from twelve of the thirteen states draft the U.S. Constitution.

George Washington

1789 George Washington becomes the first president of the United States.

1790 The temporary federal capital is moved from New York City to Philadelphia.

1791 The Bill of Rights is added to the Constitution.

1792 Thomas Jefferson forms the Republican Party to oppose the Federalist Party and to represent the rights of farmers.

1794 The U.S. and Britain sign Jay's Treaty, in which the British agree to evacuate the Great Lakes region.

1795 Congress passes the Naturalization Act, making five-year residence in the U.S. a requirement for citizenship.

1796 John Adams is elected the second U.S. president.

1798 Eli Whitney invents the concept of interchangeable musket parts, revolutionizing American and world manufacturing.
•An undeclared naval war begins between the U.S. and France.

1800 Washington D.C., becomes the new federal capital.

THE RICHES OF THE WEST

1763 In his Proclamation of 1763, King George III of Britain forbids colonists to settle west of the Appalachian Mountains in order to keep peace with the Indians, preserve the fur trade, and keep colonists within reach of British authority. The end of the French and Indian War makes it possible for many colonists still to move west.

1776 Virginia annexes Kentucky settlements. In the next several years, 20,000 new settlers arrive in Kentucky, and by 1792 the county becomes a state.

1781 Under the Act of 1781, Virginia's

poor settlers are allowed to buy 400 acres of land for 80 shillings.

1784 Spain grants trade rights in many of its ports for twenty-five years, but closes the lower Mississippi to navigation, which disrupts trade and makes

Captain Cook

settlement difficult in the area.
•Virginia gives to the Continental Congress its claims to all land north of the Ohio River.

1785 Congress passes the Land Ordinance, which authorizes the surveying of the Northwest Territory (the land between the Mississippi and Ohio rivers) and the sale of land at $1 an acre.
•Interest in the Pacific Northwest increases, following the publication of a

1801 Thomas Jefferson and Aaron Burr are tied in the U.S. presidential race; the House of Representatives chooses Jefferson as president and Burr as vice president.

1802 Congress establishes the U.S. Military Academy at West Point, New York.

1804 New England Federalists plan to form a separate northern confederacy and secede from the Union; the plan fails when Aaron Burr loses the election for the New York governorship.

1805 Jefferson is inaugurated for a second term as U.S. president; he urges Congress to spend more money on internal improvements.

1806 Britain and France, engaged in war, order naval blockades of each other's ports, seriously disrupting American shipping trade.
•Aaron Burr and Harmon Blennerhassett meet on Blennerhassett's Island to plan a military expedition to annex land in the Southwest.

1807 Congress passes the Embargo Act, which prohibits American ships from sailing into foreign ports.
•Aaron Burr is indicted for the crime of treason.
•The first commercial steamboat trip is made by Robert Fulton's *Clermont,* up the Hudson River toward Albany, New York.

Blennerhassett's mansion

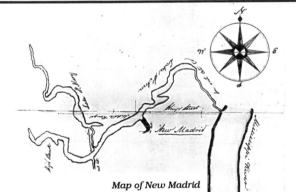

Map of New Madrid

report of Captain Cook's voyages.

1787 Congress passes the Northwest Ordinance, which calls for the Northwest Territory to eventually become three to five states, and also prohibits slavery in the region.

1789 Colonel George Morgan of Philadelphia founds the colony of New Madrid at the juncture of the Mississippi and Ohio rivers. He purchased the area from Spain.

1796 Congress passes the Land Act, which sets a minimum price for the sale of government land to settlers.

1799 The Spanish government in Louisiana grants 850 acres in Missouri to Daniel Boone.

1802 John Chapman begins his appleseed planting at Licking County, Ohio. "Johnny Appleseed" eventually plants almost 100,000 square miles of fruit-bearing trees.

1807 Fur trader Manuel Lisa leaves St. Louis to lead a trapping expedition up the Missouri River, to what is now Montana. On this journey, John Colter discovers the Yellowstone region.

A TIMELINE OF MAJOR EVENTS
1808-1845

UNITED STATES HISTORY

1809 Conceding that the Embargo Act was damaging to U.S. business, Congress passes the Non-Intercourse Act, which permits U.S. ships to trade with all countries but England and France.

1810 Construction on the Cumberland Road, which is to run from Cumberland, Maryland, to Wheeling, Ohio, begins; it is the first federally funded highway.

1812 President Madison asks Congress to declare war on Britain.
•American general William Hull and his troops are captured in Detroit by the British.

James Monroe

1813 The U.S. fleet under Captain Oliver Perry wins the Battle of Lake Erie, and the British must pull out of Detroit.
•British forces cross the Niagara River and burn Buffalo, New York.

1823 President Monroe presents his Monroe Doctrine, warning European nations not to interfere in the internal affairs of countries in the Western Hemisphere.

1830 Under the Indian Removal Act of 1830, thousands of Cherokee, Seminole, Choctaw, Creek, and Chickasaw Indians are moved from their homes in Alabama, Tennessee, Georgia, and Mississippi to Oklahoma, in what is known as the Trail of Tears; 4,000 die en route.
•Daniel Webster and Robert Hayne hold a ten-day-long senatorial debate over the issue of national union v. state's rights.

THE RICHES OF THE WEST

1808 The Missouri Fur Company is formed in St. Louis by William Clark, Manuel Lisa, and fur trader Pierre Chouteau.
•John Jacob Astor founds the American Fur Company, which will make him the richest man in the United States by the time of his death in 1848.

1811 The ship *Tonquin*, sent to the Pacific Northwest by John Jacob Astor, is destroyed by an explosion on the Columbia River, frustrating Astor's plans for a fur trading empire in the region.

1817 Julius de Mun and Pierre Chouteau move their trading and trapping business across the Spanish border, from the Arkansas River into New Mexico.

1818 The U.S. and Britain sign an agreement setting the northern boundary of the U.S. at the 49th parallel, from the Great Lakes to the Rocky Mountains. The pact opens Oregon to settlement by both nations for ten years.

1820 Congress passes the Land Act of 1820, which lowers the price of land to $1.25 an acre and the minimum purchase to eighty acres.
•William H. Ashley, the lieutenant governor of Missouri, and his partner, Andrew Henry, found the Rocky Mountain Fur Company, John Jacob Astor's main rival in the fur industry.

1821 The Prairie Schooner, an adaptation of the Conestoga wagon, is first used along the Santa Fe Trail.

1824 Jedediah Strong Smith, explorer and fur trapper for the Rocky Mountain Fur Company, leads an expedition through the Dakota

1831 Cyrus McCormick, an American inventor, develops the "reaper," a harvesting machine that revolutionizes farming in the United States and the world.
•William Lloyd Garrison founds *The Liberator*, the first anti-slavery publication to demand immediate, rather than gradual, freedom for slaves.

1833 The *New York Sun*, the first successful daily newspaper, is founded; an issue costs one penny.

1834 Abraham Lincoln enters politics for the first time, joining the assembly of the Illinois legislature; he is twenty-five years old.

1835 The national debt is completely paid off as a result of revenues from increased railroad construction and land values.

1838 The House of Representatives adopts a new "gag rule," prohibiting any discussion of the issue of slavery.

1843 Congress grants $30,000 for a trial telegraph running from Baltimore, Maryland, to Washington, D.C.

1845 Mount Holyoke, the first permanent women's college, is founded in Massachusetts.

The Liberator

Badlands, the Black Hills, and the South Pass, in what is now Wyoming.

1825 The first great "Rendezvous" is held at the Green River, in present-day Wyoming; fur trappers (known as Mountain Men) bring their year's catch to sell and trade for supplies.

1830 Congress passes the Preemption Act of 1830, which gives squatters the right to buy 160 acres of the land that they settle.
•Fierce rivalries among fur trading companies break out in Utah.

1834 Fur traders William Sublette and Robert Campbell establish Fort William, which becomes the first permanent trading post in Wyoming.

1835 The first sugar plantation in Hawaii is started by Ladd and Company on Kauai Island.

1836 Two hundred men and one hundred wagons, carrying goods worth $200,000, travel from Independence, Missouri, to Santa Fe, in Spanish territory.
•John Deere invents the steel plow.

1840 Pig iron is produced for the first time from a process using anthracite coal.

1842 The first commercial artificial fertilizer is developed.

Independence, Missouri

A TIMELINE OF MAJOR EVENTS
1846-1873

UNITED STATES HISTORY

1846 Samuel Colt receives a government contract to mass-produce revolvers for the Mexican War in his factory at Hartford, Connecticut.

1847 Abe Lincoln joins the House of Representatives.

1848 Antislavery groups form the Free Soil Party and nominate Martin Van Buren for president.
•The Pacific Mail Steamship Com-

Harriet Beecher Stowe

pany is formed to serve the growing population in the West.

1849 Congress establishes the U.S. Department of the Interior.

1850 The District of Columbia abolishes the slave trade.
•Congress passes the Fugitive Slave Act, which requires citizens of free states to return escaped slaves to their owners.

1852 *Uncle Tom's Cabin*, by Harriet Beecher Stowe, is published, arousing great sentiment against slavery.

1853 Congress passes the Coinage Act, reducing the amount of silver in all coins less than $1 and authorizing $3 gold pieces.

1854 Stephen A. Douglas introduces the Kansas-Nebraska Act in Congress; it establishes the territories of Kansas and Nebraska and advances the principle of "popular sovereignty," which asserts that each territory has the right to accept or reject slavery within its own borders.

1859 Edwin L. Drake drills the world's first oil well, in Titusville, Pennsylvania.

THE RICHES OF THE WEST

1847 Fort Benton is established in northern Montana by the American Fur Company.
•The revolving disc harrow is patented by George Page, which relieves farmers of the back-breaking task of cultivating prairie sod.

1849 Some 23,000 miners, swept up in the Gold Rush, go to California.

1850 With gold fever at its height, sailors, hoping for instant riches, desert hundreds of ships in the San Francisco Bay.

1854 The federal government opens a land office in the Kansas Territory in order to distribute property.

A Kansas Land Office

•As a result of the land obtained in the Gadsen Purchase, the first copper mine in the West opens at Ajo, in the Arizona Territory.

1858 Many settlers and miners move into the Cheyenne and Arapaho hunting grounds in Colorado, as a result of the Pikes Peak Gold Rush. The Indians refuse to sell their land and move to reservations, and Governor John Evans declares war on them, placing Colonel John Chivington in charge.
•The Comstock Lode, the richest mining discovery in U.S. history, is found in the Washoe Mountains of the Nevada Territory. The mine yields $300 million in gold and silver over the next twenty years. Virginia City is established to meet the needs of the many miners who arrive to work in the area.

1860 Abraham Lincoln is elected president, even without support from the slave states.

1861 A new Southern union, the Confederate States of America, is formed, and Jefferson Davis is chosen president.
•Telegraph wires are strung between New York City and San Francisco, making coast-to-coast communication possible for the first time.

Abraham Lincoln

1863 Lincoln issues the Emancipation Proclamation, freeing slaves in seceding states.

1865 Confederate general Robert E.

Lee surrenders to Union general Ulysses S. Grant at the Appomattox Courthouse in Virginia, ending the four-year Civil War.

1867 Congress passes the First Reconstruction Act, dividing the Southern states into five military districts.

1868 The Fourteenth Amendment, granting full citizenship to those born or naturalized in the U.S., including freed slaves, is adopted.

1869 The Fifteenth Amendment is passed in Congress, which gives black males the right to vote in both the North and the South.

1870 The Wyoming Territory passes the first law in the U.S. giving women the right to vote.

1873 The Coinage Act of 1873 is passed by Congress, making gold the sole U.S. monetary standard.

1862 President Abraham Lincoln signs the Homestead Act, which gives settlers 160-acre parcels for free once they have settled them for five years.

1865 The Union Stockyard opens in Chicago, leading the way for the development of other stockraising and railroad industries across the West.

1867 The Grange, formerly known as the Patrons of Husbandry, is founded in Washington, D.C., to support agricultural interests.

1869 James Oliver patents the chilled-iron plow, which breaks through the tough prairie soil without clogging.

1872 Congress establishes Yellowstone Park in Wyoming, to help conserve the nation's natural resources.

1873 Congress passes the Timber Culture Act, which grants a person who plants forty acres of trees an additional 160 acres of land.
•Barbed wire, which will be used extensively for fences on the open prairie, is manufactured by Joseph F. Glidden, in De Kalb, Illinois.
•The richest gold strike in history is made by four miners digging the "Big Bonanza" at Davidson Mountain, near Virginia City, Nevada.

Mining on the Comstock Lode

A TIMELINE OF MAJOR EVENTS
1874-1910

UNITED STATES HISTORY

1875 Congress passes the Civil Rights Act, guaranteeing blacks equal rights in public places.

1877 The last federal troops stationed in the South are withdrawn from New Orleans, and

Chinese laborers

the Southern states regain control of their governments.

1878 Labor organizations join with advocates of paper money to form the Greenback-Labor Party.

1880 The National Farmers' Alliance is formed in Chicago to unite farmers against discriminatory legislation.

1882 Congress passes the Chinese Exclusion Act, prohibiting Chinese laborers from entering the U.S. for ten years.

1883 Indiscriminate tree cutting and wasteful farming methods lead to severe flooding of the Ohio River; damage in the area amounts to millions of dollars.

1886 Congress passes the Presidential Succession Act, which provides for the succession of the president or vice president in the event that one dies while still in office.

1887 Congress passes the Dawes Act, which divides reservation land into plots of 160 acres; the extra land is opened to white settlers.

1890 The National Women's Suffrage Association is formed in an effort to win women the right to vote in national elections.

1891 Immigration to the U.S. greatly increases as

THE RICHES OF THE WEST

1874 Clouds of grasshoppers destroy crops, trees, and farm equipment, from Texas to the Canadian border, during the worst grasshopper plague in history.
•Deadwood, a mining town in the Dakota Territory that becomes an example of frontier lawlessness, is founded.

1877 Congress passes the Desert Land Act, which offers a person 640 acres of land at $1.25 per acre, provided the person agrees to irrigate some portion of the land.

1878 Congress passes the Timber and Stone Act, which allows timber to be cut on public land in an effort to increase the amount of farm land; most of the land, however, is given or sold to timber interests.

1885 Congress passes an act which forbids the fencing of public lands in the West.

1886 Eastern markets receive the first shipments of California fruit, launching the agricultural business on the West Coast.

1889 The Department of Agriculture is organized to supervise the growth of agriculture in the West.

1891 Winfield Scott Stratton discovers gold near Denver, Colorado, in the Cripple Creek field of the Rocky Mountains. The gold, worth millions, makes Stratton one of the legendary Bonanza Kings of Cripple Creek.

1897 Miners discover a rich vein of lead and silver when they reopen a deserted mineshaft in the town of Leadville, Colorado.
•Oil is discovered in Bartsville, Oklahoma. Oil becomes the area's biggest industry as more

560,319 immigrants arrive from abroad.

1892 President Harrison opens 3 million acres of Cheyenne and Arapaho land in Oklahoma to white settlers.

1896 The Supreme Court rules in *Plessy* v. *Ferguson* that "separate but equal" facilities for blacks and whites are constitutional.

1901 U.S. citizenship is granted to the Cherokee, Creek, Choctaw, Chickasaw, and Seminole Indian tribes.
•The U.S. and Britain sign the Hay-Paunceforte Treaty, giving the U.S. the right to build and operate a canal across the isthmus of Panama.
•Anarchist Leon Czolgosz shoots and kills President McKinley at Buffalo, New York. Theodore Roosevelt becomes president.

1904 The Supreme Court rules that Puerto Ricans, while not U.S. citizens, are not considered aliens.

1905 President Roosevelt helps Russia and Japan negotiate a treaty to end the Russo-Japanese War and wins the Nobel Peace Prize for his efforts.

W E. B. DuBois

1907 U.S. Marines land in Honduras to help put down a revolution and to protect U.S. interests in that region.

1908 Automaker Henry Ford introduces the Model T, the first mass-produced car in the world.

1910 Black leader W. E. B. DuBois founds the National Association for the Advancement of Colored People (N.A.A.C.P.).

---

strikes are made over the next several decades.

1900 In Tonopah, Nevada, both gold and silver deposits are discovered, touching off a new rush of prospectors to the region.

1901 A dispute between cattle ranchers and sheepherders erupts into violence that lasts five years. In Wyoming, masked men kill many sheep herds, and several murders are attributed to cattlemen.

1904 The Kirkland Act grants 640 acres of desert land in Nebraska to farmers willing to spend five years improving the land.

A cattle raid

1905 The first of two major mine disasters occurs at Mine Number One of the Union Pacific Mine at Hanna, Wyoming; 171 men are killed in the explosion. Another sixty men perish in a cave in 1908.

1910 Major dams are constructed to bring water to new areas: the Shoshone Dam in Wyoming is completed in 1910, and Theodore Roosevelt presides at the opening of the Roosevelt Dam in Arizona the next year.

Part I
Seizing the Resources of the West

Frederic Remington's print, "Hauling Logs to the River," first appeared in a 1907 issue of Collier's *magazine. Remington originally called the print "The Tragedy of the Trees, Part III," seeing it as a symbol of the destruction of the wilderness.* Collier's, *however, renamed the painting to express human triumph over nature.*

The great appeal of the West was its wealth of resources. Several wars were fought on American soil as various powers struggled over control of the Western frontier. The competition between British and French fur traders for the fur-rich lands in the Ohio River Valley led to the French and Indian War (1754–63). After the American Revolution, the struggle between Americans and British in Canada for control of the lands surrounding the Great Lakes contributed to the War of 1812. A treaty in 1818 fixed the U.S.-Canadian border at the 49th parallel from the Lake of the Woods to the Rocky Mountains. In 1803, the Louisiana Purchase encouraged further movement westward, into the wilderness beyond the Mississippi, by pioneers hoping to find their fortunes in the West.

Because of the huge population of fur-bearing animals—especially beavers—fur trading, hunting, and trapping became the first profitable industries in what some Europeans called the "New Golden Land." By the middle of the nineteenth century, with the West "trapped out," pioneers turned to other resources. The wealth of minerals—especially gold and silver, but also lead, iron, copper, and zinc—attracted a flood of fortune seekers to the West. The quest for timber also drew settlers farther and farther westward as the forests of the East were cleared for settlements.

In 1912, when New Mexico and Arizona became the forty-seventh and forty-eighth states admitted to the Union, westward expansion ended. The United States had truly become a land that stretched "from sea to shining sea."

The territory claimed by the United States grew dramatically between the signing of the Declaration of Independence in 1776 and the Alaska Purchase in 1867. By the time of the Louisiana Purchase in 1803, four new states (Vermont, Kentucky, Tennessee, and Ohio) had already been admitted to join the original thirteen states. The Louisiana Purchase—828,000 square miles for $15 million—doubled the size of the United States and began the great surge into the West.

As westward expansion made ports on the Gulf of Mexico desirable, the United States set out to acquire Florida from Spain. In 1819, a treaty granted Florida and all the Gulf Coast lands to the United States. In 1846, a treaty with Great Britain fixed the northern border of the United States at the 49th parallel all the way to the West Coast. The northwest corner of the United States became known as the Oregon Country. After defeating Mexico in a war over the annexation of Texas in 1848, the United States acquired most of the territory that today makes up California and the southwestern United States. The Gadsden Purchase in 1853, which added southern Arizona and southern New Mexico, fixed the borders of the continental United States. By 1867, the original thirteen states had grown to thirty-seven states, plus nine continental territories and Alaska.

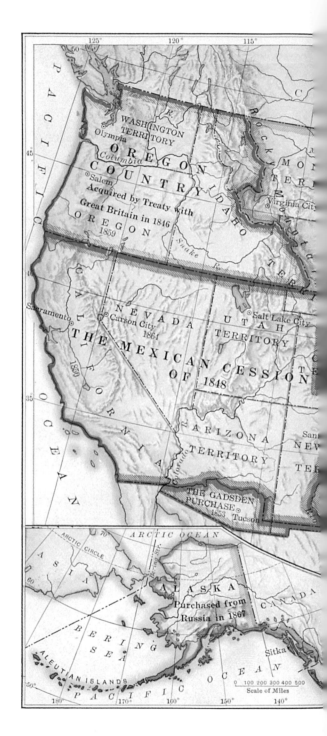

THE GROWTH
of the
UNITED STATES
From 1776 to 1867

The acquisitions made by the United States from
1776 to 1867 are shown by different colors.

The boundaries of the States and Territories at the close
of 1867 are outlined by solid green lines:

The Capitals of the States and Territories
in 1867 are shown on map by: ⊙

0	100	200	400	600

Scale of Miles

THE M.-N. WORKS.

INTO THE
WILDERNESS

As early as the seventeenth century, the quest for furs fueled the push into the American wilderness. In 1763, when the French and Indian War ended, the overwhelming British victory forced France to withdraw all territorial claims on the continent. French trappers remained, but they were now isolated on the fur-rich lands dominated by the British.

Native Americans, meanwhile, were justifiably angered by high British prices for trade goods and by the intrusion of settlers who were driving them off their traditional hunting grounds. They posed a constant danger for traders and trappers. In 1763, Pontiac (c.1720–69), chief of the Ottawas, united virtually all of the tribes from Lake Superior to the lower Mississippi Valley. Pontiac's Rebellion attempted to destroy all British trading posts and drive settlers out of the region.

The rebellion failed, and conflict with Native Americans died down somewhat, allowing British fur traders and trappers to expand the fur trade. They established trading posts in the land east of the Mississippi as well as in the land then known as the Northwest Territory—the Great Lakes region. After the Revolutionary War, these lands came under U.S. control. Led by John Jacob Astor (1763–1848), who eventually made a fortune in fur-trading, Americans took over British trading posts on the Great Lakes. Trappers and traders continued to play an important role in expanding the frontier for the next hundred years.

This map (opposite, top) shows the region known as the Northwest Territory. This fur-rich land, a focus of British-American disputes for forty years, was also defended by the most powerful of all Indian alliances: the Five Nations of the Iroquois Confederacy.

Except for isolated explorers, trappers and traders were virtually the only whites who ventured very far west of the Mississippi River before the Mexican War (1846–48). Pioneering European fur traders (opposite, bottom) were joined and eventually replaced by American trappers, who cut out the middleman by capturing their own furs instead of trading for them.

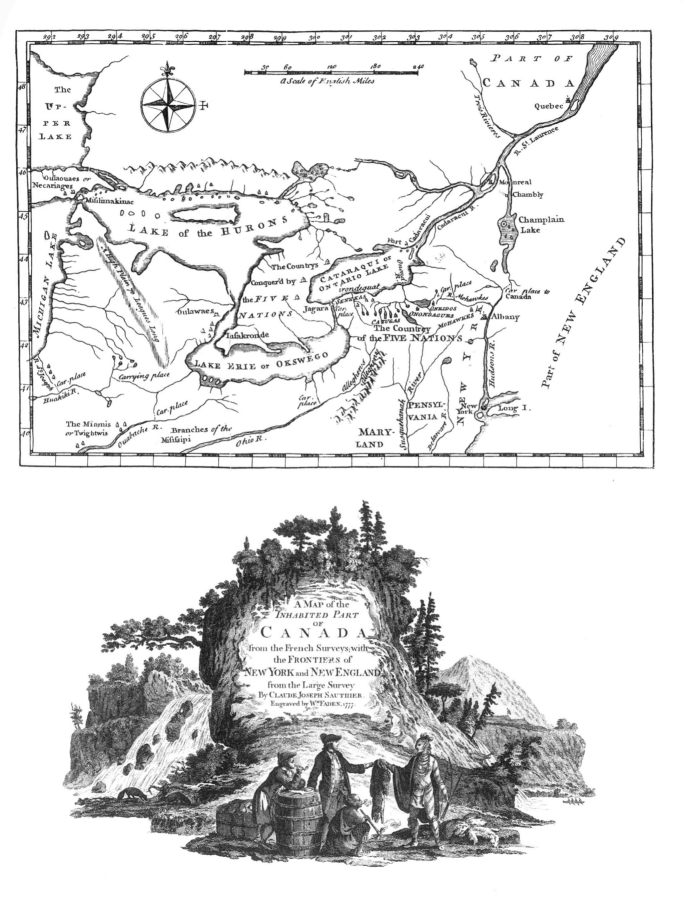

FRONTIER LIFE

Before the Civil War (1861–65), most of the Western heartland acquired through the Louisiana Purchase in 1803 remained unsettled. At that time, the land between the Appalachian Mountains and the Mississippi River was considered the frontier. Pioneers, including many immigrants to the United States, eventually pushed westward, however, to settle beyond the Mississippi. The main attractions were cheap land and rich resources—chiefly furs at first. By the middle of the nineteenth century, precious metals had begun to attract miners.

Life on the frontier posed many difficulties. Nature itself challenged the pioneers with floods, rushing rivers, harsh winters, snowslides, and dangerous wildlife. In addition, there was the risk of violence from Native Americans who were defending their lands. With no nearby towns or cities to fall back on, the pioneers faced these dangers alone. They were further isolated by the absence of roads, which made it difficult to travel and bring in supplies or send out goods for sale. Yet these treacherous conditions helped foster independence, courage, and self-reliance—the qualities that became identified with the pioneers who opened up the American frontier.

Frontier legend Davy Crockett (1786–1836) defined a backwoodsman as "a singular being always moving westward like a buffalo before the tide of civilization. He does not want a neighbor nearer than ten miles." Squatters, shown in this illustration (opposite, top), were often evicted from the land by the government because squatting—settling on public land not yet up for sale—was illegal until 1830.

Finding it nearly impossible to transport building supplies into the wilderness, the pioneers made do with what materials were available. Using nothing more than an ax, pioneers could build a one-room log cabin, as shown in this 1796 sketch (opposite, bottom)—filling the spaces between logs with moss, mud, or manure—in about two weeks.

Clashes with Native Americans posed a danger
even to the earliest of pioneers. Shown here in
this painting by Howard Pyle (above) is the
famous capture of Betsey and Frances (Fanny)
Calloway in 1776. Frontier adventurer Daniel
Boone (1734–1820) rescued the sisters, along
with his daughter Jemima, after Indians had
carried them off when they tried to cross the river
opposite Boonesborough—the first permanent
white settlement in Kentucky.

As this 1861 lithograph shows, the most fearsome wildlife predators faced by pioneers and trappers were the grizzly bears, who would sometimes attack human beings. Hunters and trappers lucky enough to survive grizzly attacks often suffered horrific cuts, torn flesh, crushed ribs, and broken bones.

REWARDS THAT SURPASSED THE RISKS

In 1806, when Meriwether Lewis (1774–1809) and William Clark (1770–1838) returned from their historic trek across the continent, they brought back reports of enormous populations of fur-bearing animals on the Missouri River and its headwaters in the Rockies. To ambitious and enterprising trappers, the dangers of animal attacks, Indian hostilities, and the rigors of the wilderness climate seemed trivial in comparison to the potentially vast riches of the fur trade. From the Missouri River, trappers broke trails westward through the Dakotas and then south through the Rocky Mountain river valleys. They trapped fur-bearing animals such as foxes, bears, deer, and muskrats. But the pelt that brought the greatest return was that of the beaver.

Most trappers and traders were hired on a commission basis by highly competitive fur companies such as the British Hudson's Bay Company, the Pacific Fur Company, and the huge American Fur Company—the last two founded by John Jacob Astor. The potential rewards were enormous: The fur trade earned between $200,000 and $300,000 annually from 1807 to 1847. Astor himself sold his fur interests in 1834, years before the fur trade began to sag. He accumulated a fortune of more than $20 million before he died, making him the richest man in America.

An adult beaver like the one in this engraving (left) yielded a pelt weighing one or two pounds that would sell for around $5. Trappers would bait and set their traps in the water, drowning the beaver. The trapper would then skin the beaver, remove a gland that would be used as bait for the next trap, and char and boil the tail—considered a delicacy in the wilderness.

After gathering a rich cargo of pelts in the winter, trappers and traders needed to return to St. Louis—gateway to the West and center of the fur trade—in the spring. Yet along the Missouri, Native Americans—especially members of the Blackfoot and Arikara tribes—posed a constant threat to trappers, depicted vividly in this 1868 sketch by W. M. Cary (below).

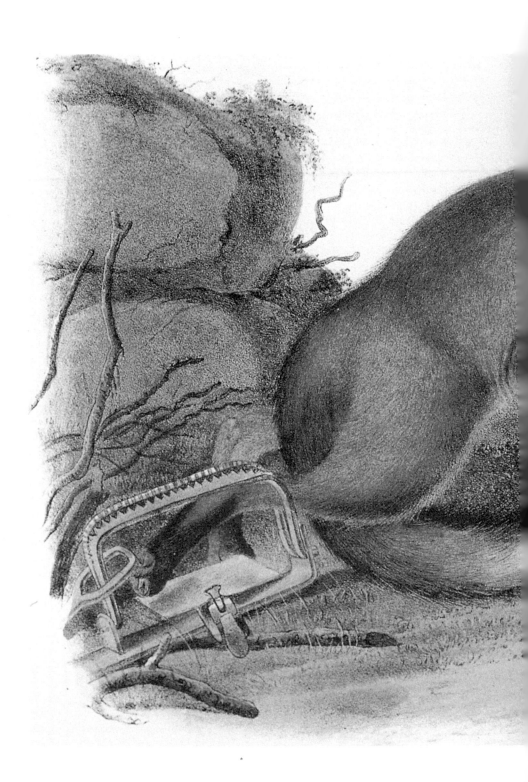

Although trappers preferred hunting for beaver, many also turned a profit catching other animals, such as the American red fox. This engraving by naturalist John J. Audubon (1785–1851) portrays the agony of a fox whose leg has been caught in a metal trap.

THE FAR WILDERNESS

The most prized region of the "trans-Mississippi" wilderness was the Oregon Country, which stretched from the Rockies to the Pacific and included what is now Idaho, Washington, and British Columbia. Under an 1818 treaty, the region was jointly occupied by British and American settlers. British trappers employed by the Hudson's Bay Company worked in large groups, using frontier outposts as headquarters. The British hoped to discourage American competition in the region by exhausting the Oregon Country's rich supply of fur-bearing animals. Unfortunately, the strategy succeeded only in decimating the beaver population.

American trappers, unlike their British counterparts, worked alone or in small groups, with no military support and few frontier forts. Over the next twenty years, 3,000 trappers and traders staked claims and broke trails, paving the way for settlers, 900 of whom arrived in Oregon in 1843. But the founding of permanent settlements, combined with the thinning of the beaver population, brought to an end the days of the free and adventurous Mountain Man.

The Mountain Men, like the one in this 1888 engraving from Harper's magazine (right), were hardy individualists who survived in the wilderness by living much as the Native Americans did. After opening up the West and trapping out the richest beaver streams, many Mountain Men served as trail guides for settlers and as scouts for the army.

Fort Nez Perce, established in 1818 by the British and shown in this 1855 lithograph (below), was a typical frontier outpost for British trappers and traders in the Oregon Country. Since Native Americans were almost never admitted inside the walls of the fort, all trading was done through an iron gate in the wall. This outpost in southeastern Washington was later called Fort Walla Walla.

WHERE THE BUFFALO ROAM

By the late 1830s, Mountain Men had killed off so much of the beaver population that trapping became increasingly difficult and profits steadily declined. Trading with the Indians for buffalo skins became more important. The Plains Indians had long hunted American buffalo, or bison, for meat, using their fur for winter robes and their hides for tepees. White hunters, led by the American Fur Company, began killing buffalo in larger numbers in the 1840s. The demand for buffalo hides increased after tanners discovered that they provided a good source of leather. Buffalo meat was also popular, providing a mainstay of the diet of hunters on the Great Plains. Although Native American hunters would eat the raw liver and some other parts of the buffalo immediately after killing the beasts, most white hunters boiled or roasted meat from the hump, or dried thin slices of meat and mixed it with melted fat to make "pemmican," a food that traveled well.

Buffalo were abundant in the Great Plains of Kansas, Iowa, Nebraska, Oklahoma, and Texas. An estimated 75 million buffalo lived on the Plains in 1810, before the Indians began acquiring horses and the whites began killing buffalo for sport. With so many buffalo available, no one thought that they would ever disappear from the Plains.

This nineteenth-century lithograph (below) entitled "Herd of Bison Near Lake Jessie" shows the impressive buffalo herds which were so large that they sometimes covered the entire countryside as far as the eye could see. Westward-bound pioneers sometimes needed to wait half a day or more for a herd to thunder past and clear the road for travel.

Buffalo hunters, like those in this 1862 illustration (below), would enter a herd and then chase the animals at full gallop. In order to save money on bullets, they would fire their rifles at close range, hoping for a kill with every bullet. A hunter could easily kill fifty animals in a day.

One of the great dangers on the Great Plains was fire, which in the hot summer months could quickly sweep across the dry, treeless grassland. As in this Arthur Tait illustration (above), pioneers would build a firebreak to combat fire, deliberately burning off the grass along a strip of land in order to prevent the fire from spreading.

KILL AND MOVE ON

As the frontier moved steadily westward, the once vast herds of buffalo were shrinking rapidly. Not only did pioneering settlers drive the massive herds off the land, but hunters had begun killing them for sport. Although the herds had once seemed too numerous to disappear, guns destroyed the herds at a greater rate than bows and arrows, and guns were now used by both whites and Native Americans. Having virtually destroyed the herds in the central Plains by the early 1870s, hunters began moving into Texas, giving little thought to the fact that these hunting grounds had been reserved for Native Americans by treaty.

In the course of a decade, hunters wiped out the southern herds too, scattering the surviving buffalo population. Millions upon millions were killed, reducing the population of buffalo to a few small herds on the northern Plains by the early 1880s. With their primary source of meat, shelter, and clothing destroyed, the Native Americans on the Plains became much more dependent on whites, and their hunting grounds gave way to enormous cattle ranches.

Sport hunters, seen here shooting buffalo from the top of a moving train (above), would sometimes leave a trail of dead animals that stretched for miles and miles through the prairie.

This depiction of hunters skinning buffalo appeared on the cover of Harper's Weekly *in 1874 (right). Native American buffalo hunters had used virtually every part of their kill for food, housing, clothing, and even tools. Those hunters who killed only for the hides, however, usually left the skinned carcasses strewn along the prairies, where the meat would feed other animals or rot.*

NATURAL RESOURCES AND THE NATIVE AMERICANS

At first, Indians were willing partners in the fur trade. They became used to the blankets, metal knives, cooking pots, and firearms the fur trade provided and lost the ability to survive independently. Dependent on traders, they were vulnerable to being cheated, especially if intoxicated—and alcohol was a staple of trade. Contact with Europeans also brought devastating epidemics. Soon, abusive hunting, especially of beaver and buffalo, led to the near extinction of the animals and threatened the Indians with starvation.

Eventually the Indians were pushed from their native lands to make way for white settlers. Treaties forced upon the Indians took away their land and the rights to its resources, including minerals, fish, and game. Indians were relocated to reservations, often in less fertile areas, where they were compelled to become farmers.

Demands by whites for Indian lands accelerated when valuable silver and gold deposits were found. Rumors of gold were enough to provoke confrontations in the Black Hills, sacred to the Sioux tribes, which led to the famous Battle of Little Bighorn in 1876. The Indian wars continued until the massacre at Wounded Knee in 1890.

The Plains Indians depended on the buffalo for their survival, and their lives changed dramatically when the buffalo population dwindled at the hands of white hunters. This engraving (left), based on a painting by Frederic Remington, shows a romanticized view of the aftermath: An Indian brave holds a buffalo skull above his head, perhaps to conjure back the enormous herds of the past.

Despite the prohibition against bringing liquor into Indian lands, many traders were unscrupulous about trading liquor for pelts. Some traders would even go so far as to get Indians drunk (below) in order to cheat them of their furs.

IN CALIFORNIA

In the first half of the nineteenth century, most of California was part of the great Western wilderness. With the exception of the twenty-one Spanish missions established in the last half of the eighteenth century, very few Europeans had made California their home. When Mexico gained independence from Spain in 1821, California became a Mexican territory. The California missions, which under the direction of the Spanish *padres* (priests) had become small centers for farming, fell into the hands of prominent Mexicans. For the next twenty-five years, "Californios" (Mexicans of Spanish descent) and Native Americans would make up most of the population in the territory.

The landscape of this Californian wilderness offered great variety, with mountains, deserts, and forests located within a dozen miles of one another. The mountains and deserts in eastern California made overland travel to the territory difficult. Nonetheless, by 1841 American settlers began arriving in wagon trains from the East. These hardy settlers declared California a republic independent of Mexico in 1846. As part of the Mexican War that followed, Californios surrendered to troops under the command of John C. Frémont in January, 1847. One year later, with the discovery of gold, the character of the California wilderness would change completely.

In this 1873 engraving, three riders employed by Spanish mission ranchers work together to lasso a dangerous grizzly bear. For sport, the captured bear would then be pitted against the strongest bull on the ranch in a brutal fight to the death.

"FORTY-NINERS" RUSH WESTWARD

In January 1848, James Marshall (1810–85), a carpenter who was building a sawmill for John Sutter (1803–80), discovered a nugget of gold about the size of a dime. This accidental discovery set off the most feverish gold rush in history. Sutter, who owned the land near the junction of the American and Sacramento rivers, tried to keep the discovery quiet. His attempt at secrecy was foiled by Sam Brannan (1819–99), an enterprising businessman who owned a general store a few miles from Sutter's Mill. Brannan, seeing an opportunity to round up new customers for his store, went to San Francisco with a bottle of gold dust and shouted in the streets, "Gold! Gold from the American River!"

The Gold Rush drew thousands of optimistic prospectors to California in the hope of getting rich quickly. The population of California swelled from less than 20,000 in 1848 to almost 250,000 four years later. Although the California Gold Rush is by far the best known, many others—in Colorado, Nevada, Idaho, Montana, and the Dakotas—would follow. Indeed, the smallest amount of gold discovered in a creek bed could set off a frenzy of incoming prospectors. Although almost $750 million worth of gold was mined in California by 1865, many prospectors not only failed to make their fortunes, but also lost everything they had.

Miners working in groups proved much more successful than prospectors trying to work alone. This 1871 Currier & Ives lithograph (right) shows many different types of gold mining. Those in the foreground are using a wooden basin called a sluice and a metal pan to separate gold flakes from sand, dirt, and clay from the creek bed. Those in the background are using picks to dig out gold from the surrounding soil.

Attracted by exaggerated reports of gold in the region, 100,000 prospectors set out for Colorado in 1859. Traveling in wagon trains like the one in this engraving (below) marked "Bound to Pikes Peak" or "Pikes Peak or Bust," they headed west in pursuit of a land hailed as "New Eldorado," the legendary city of gold. Only half arrived, the rest turning back, getting lost, or dying of disease, hunger, or thirst. In the next decade, Colorado would surpass California as the nation's leading producer of gold.

HOW TO DIG GOLD

When staking a new claim, prospectors would start looking for gold in streambeds, because this did not require any costly equipment. Those streambeds in the foothills of mountain ranges, where the current would slow down and heavier gold deposits would settle, produced especially rich yields. If a prospector found a rich stream, he might team up with other prospectors to build sluices—a much more efficient means of separating gold from silt. Ambitious prospectors might dig down several inches or even several feet into a creek bed trying to find the bedrock where gold would ultimately settle.

The next step would involve trying to locate the mother lode—the source of the gold that had been brought down the river by erosion. Prospectors would follow the creek upstream, hoping to find the vein of quartz in which the gold was embedded. However, prospectors lucky enough to find a rich lode often found that they did not have the financial resources to develop and exploit their mines. They would often sell their mines to wealthy developers or large mining companies that could afford to drill deep tunnels, hire the miners to chip away at the ore, build the mills, and buy the heavy machinery needed to separate rock from gold.

Lone prospectors, like these three in the Dakota Territory (above), would most often separate gold from soil by "panning." After using a pan to collect sand from a creek bed, the prospector would let water wash over it. When the method worked, the gold (eight times heavier than sand) would sink to the bottom while the sand would get washed out of the pan. Since smaller flakes of gold would also wash away, however, a lot of gold was lost using this method.

Mining the ore was only half the job, once a lode had been discovered. The quartz still needed to be crushed in order to separate the gold from the rock that encased it. Mining companies and wealthy investors built mills like this one (below) on the slopes of hills not far from their lode mines.

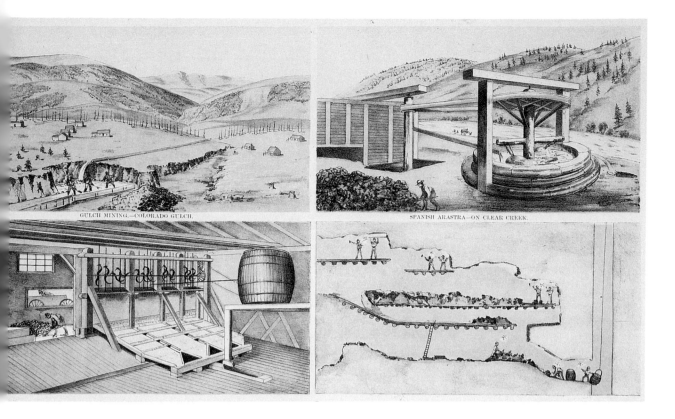

GULCH MINING.—COLORADO GULCH.

SPANISH ARASTRA—ON CLEAR CREEK.

This four part sketch (above) shows some of the machinery used to mill gold. Gravel-washing machines known as sluices or cradles (upper left) could separate dirt from gold dust much more efficiently than could a single miner with a pan. Slats nailed across the bottoms of the sluices would trap much of the gold. Liquid mercury—which causes gold and silver (but not rock) to dissolve and attach to the mercury—was used to catch finer particles of gold.

The arastra (upper right), a water-powered machine that dragged heavy, flat boulders across chunks of quartz in order to pulverize them, was used to separate gold from the rock that surrounded it. The pulverized stone and metal dust would then be washed into a sluice, where the gold could be separated from the stone by sluicing, panning, or combining with mercury.

Steam or water-powered stamp mills (lower left) used powerful iron stamps that rose and fell like pile drivers to crush hard ore into powder. Water would then wash the powder through small holes, then over copper tables covered with mercury, which would catch whatever gold escaped the box.

When large mining companies bought the claim to a lode, they would build shaft mines. Deep vertical or inclined shafts would lead to tunnels where hired miners dug or blasted the ore. The Colorado shaft pictured here (lower right) was 350 feet deep and four and a half feet wide. Some miners would dig holes to prepare for blasting, while others shoveled blasted ore to the shaft, where steam-powered lifts would carry it to the surface.

SILVER AND LEAD MINING

Prospectors in the West became so eager to find gold that many completely ignored other sources of wealth at their fingertips: lead, copper, zinc, and most important, silver. Silver, though valuable, was much harder for miners to spot. The white metal took on a dark blue color when combined with gold, a pitch black color when combined with lead, and other shades when mixed with other minerals. This made it impossible for prospectors to know the concentration of silver in a particular sample—and therefore whether the area was worth mining—without first taking it to an assayer (a metals analyst). Silver was also harder to mine. Miners needed to dig ore, pulverize it, and separate silver in the same manner in which gold was mined—and this kind of operation cost a lot of money up front.

Despite these difficulties and the fact that gold sold for ten times more per ounce than silver, the high concentration of silver in lodes often made them much more valuable than individual gold lodes. Although rich deposits of silver were found in Colorado, southern Arizona, and Idaho, the greatest silver deposit was found in Nevada. The legendary Comstock Lode, discovered in 1859 in Nevada's Washoe Mountains, quickly became the richest source of silver in the world. The lode, rich in gold as well, yielded over $100 million in silver alone in twenty years. By 1890, it had produced almost $400 million in silver and gold.

Miners employed by Virginia City's Savage Mine are shown here (above) preparing to descend into a shaft in order to mine the Comstock Lode. The miners, some wheeling ore cars in front of them, will be carried down to horizontal tunnels hundreds of feet below the ground.

This 1861 lithograph (opposite, top) shows Nevada's first and greatest mining town, Virginia City—with detailed illustrations of prominent saloons, hotels, stores, and residences in the border. Within just a few years of the 1859 discovery of the Comstock Lode, the population of Virginia City had boomed to 20,000 people.

This 1862 map of the Nevada Territory's silver region (opposite, bottom) includes all of the area's first mining towns (with Virginia City located at the top, center of the map). It also names various mining districts, details individual claims, and lists (in the inset, lower right) all mining companies working on the Comstock Lode.

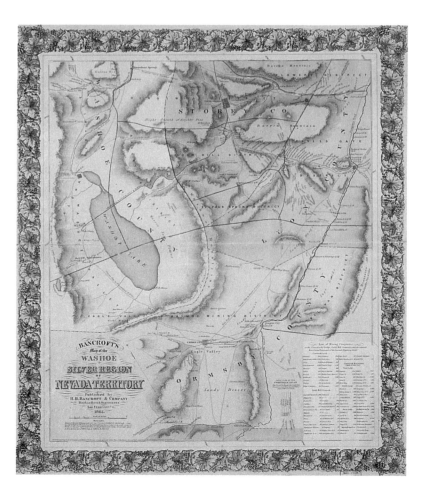

THE BIRTH OF MINING TOWNS

Any mineral vein that seemed promising quickly attracted scores of competing prospectors and miners to the area. Next came wagons loaded with supplies and goods for sale, followed by storekeepers, bartenders, gamblers, and prostitutes. Dozens of these mining boomtowns—drawing a diverse population of Americans from the East, as well as Mexicans, Spanish, Native Americans, and Chinese—rose quickly throughout the West. One important segment of the population was scarce, however. With the exception of traveling dance-hall performers and prostitutes, few women were seen in the rough mining camps and towns. Only after the towns had become well established would women arrive as permanent settlers.

Boomtowns with populations of around 20,000—such as Virginia City, Nevada, and Leadville, Colorado—commonly had more than one hundred saloons. Crimes such as drunk and disorderly conduct, disturbing the peace, and fighting occurred frequently. The boomtowns generally enforced their own laws, punishing more serious crimes such as violence or robbery with beatings or hangings, since jails were scarce. Towns often went boom and then bust within ten years or less. When the gold and silver disappeared from the mines, the population often did, too. Except for a few towns that later drew permanent settlers, boomtowns often turned into ghost towns as quickly as they had risen.

This humorous lithograph (above) depicts a group of prospectors welcoming a rare sight: the arrival of a young woman in their mining town. Since women seldom visited the mining towns, the prospectors' expressions betray their delight when they hear that she is unmarried.

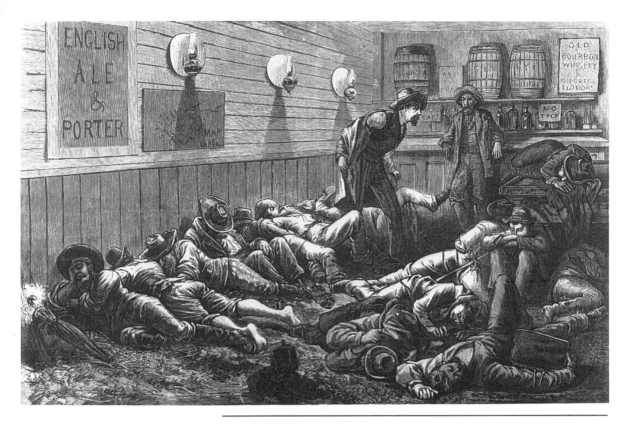

Leadville, Colorado, a typical boomtown, grew from a handful of prospectors in 1877 to 20,000 miners just two years later when this sketch was published in Leslie's magazine (above). By this time, Leadville already had nearly a hundred saloons. Arriving miners could either pitch a tent or, as these chose to do, sleep on the floor of a saloon for 25 cents a night.

This sketch (right), which appeared in Harper's Weekly in 1875, shows what happened to mining camps once the gold disappeared. Miners had ambitiously constructed log cabins, sluices, and dams along this mountain stream in Colorado. Just a year later, however, the miners had abandoned their cabins, let their sluices rot away, and allowed the stream to resume its original course. The gold had run out.

FROM MINING TOWNS TO RICH CITIES

In addition to creating mining boom-towns, the rush to the West for gold and silver also helped build thriving cities. Several mining camps eventually grew into cities, most notably Boise, Idaho, and Helena, Montana. But the settlements most likely to mature into prosperous cities were not the mining towns themselves, but rather the supply towns where miners would purchase the equipment needed for their mining operations, as well as their food, clothing, and liquor. These towns were quickly overrun with storekeepers, bartenders, hotel-keepers, assayers, bankers, investors, lawyers, gamblers, thieves, and con artists—all looking to make a buck off of successful prospectors.

The greatest metropolis was San Francisco, the gateway to the mining country, which became the fastest-growing city in the world in the 1850s. Newcomers from all over the world arrived in the port city, where they bought supplies before moving into the hills to find gold. Supplies, food, and lodging did not come cheap in this city. Prospectors could pay up to $8 a night for a cot in a crowded room, $1 apiece for eggs, and $40 for a quart of whiskey. With so much money and so many people competing for it, the city also became infamous for its lawlessness. Murder, arson, and robbery were daily occurrences.

A village of just 800 people before the Gold Rush, San Francisco grew to 5,000 by 1849, to almost 25,000 by 1850, and to 50,000 by 1860. Ramshackle wooden buildings were extremely vulnerable to fires, three of which devastated the city in 1850 alone. Over 200 abandoned vessels seen in the distance in this Francis Marryat drawing (right) littered the harbor by July 1849.

This illustration (below) shows busy Blake Street in Denver. Originally just a way station for trappers, traders, and Native Americans prior to the 1859 Colorado Gold Rush, it became a boomtown overnight. Although designated as the permanent capital of the Colorado Territory in 1867, Denver had grown to only 5,000 people by 1870. Once connected with the East by the Kansas Pacific Railroad, however, the population exploded, exceeding 100,000 by 1890.

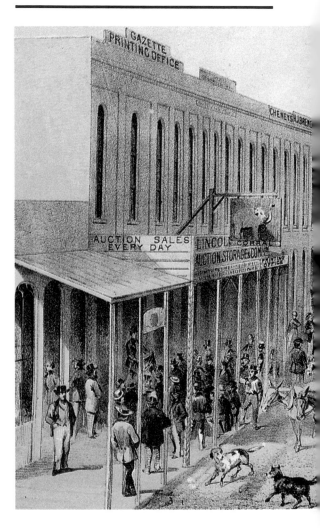

TAKING FROM THE GREAT FORESTS

In addition to fur-bearing animals and precious metals, the West had yet another rich resource to offer: trees. With the forests of the East already stripped, American loggers headed westward. Trees were especially important to those eager to settle an area. Pioneers chopped down trees to build not only furniture, but houses, walls, floors, and fences as well. Those who wanted to settle on the treeless Western prairies therefore needed to import timber from the tree-rich regions to the north and farther west.

Logging was done by hand in the nineteenth century. During the winter months, loggers used axes to fell trees, cross-cut them into logs, chop off their branches, and peel their bark. Horse-drawn sleds would then carry the logs to a frozen river. When the river thawed in the spring, the logs would float downriver to a regional sawmill. Western loggers remained entirely unrestrained by law until 1891, when Congress authorized the president to set aside reserves of forested land for the public domain. Nonetheless, loggers took a huge chunk of the nation's forests. California, for example, had an estimated 1.5 million acres of redwoods prior to European settlement. Only 109,000 acres remain as protected forests today.

The process of moving cut and trimmed logs from the felling site to the river that would carry them to the sawmill was called skidding. This lithograph (right) shows a single team of horses skidding a tremendous load out of the Michigan woods.

The nation's Sequoia forests featured trees of awe-inspiring size. Photographer Darius Kinsey counted the rings of this massive tree (below) and claimed it was 129 years older than Methuselah, the biblical character reputed to have lived 969 years.

The size of redwood trees in California is astonishing. This 1905 photograph (left) shows a horse-drawn carriage passing through a tunnel carved in a giant California redwood trunk.

General John C. Frémont, who had led the armed forces that captured California from Mexico forty-two years earlier, returned to the site of his California military headquarters two years before his death. There, Frémont, the man with the white beard standing closest to the tree, and a group of friends posed for the photograph (above), demonstrating the enormous circumference of the redwood behind them by joining hands in a circle.

Part II

Living Off the Land

Throughout the late eighteenth and into the nineteenth centuries, the United States government was eager to establish a permanent presence in the West, and it introduced policies intended to lure settlers westward. Following territorial gains made as a result of the War of 1812, in 1820 the U.S. government set the price of land at $1.25 an acre, and the minimum purchase at 80 acres. For $100 pioneers could buy a farm.

To avoid the high costs, many pioneers became squatters—clearing the land of trees and planting crops on public land that they then called their own. The government legalized squatting with the Preemption Act of 1830, which allowed squatters to buy up to 160 acres of land for a minimum of $1.25 an acre. The law that really opened up the West to ranchers and farmers, however, was the Homestead Act, rushed through Congress during the Civil War in 1862. It offered 160 acres of public land free to anyone willing to settle on it for at least five years.

Farmers remained skeptical about the quality of land on the desolate prairie. But cattle ranchers and sheepherders quickly took advantage of the abundant grasslands that allowed them to feed their animals for free. Their success convinced a flood of homesteaders that the land could support them, too.

By the end of the century, hundreds of thousands of pioneering farmers had settled all the way across the Plains and throughout the fertile valleys along the Pacific. Most found that they could support their families by living off the land. And by doing so, they established permanent settlements all the way across the continent.

This painting by Olaf Seltzer, titled "Return of the Bolters," shows a cowboy trying to round up some stray cattle that have broken away from the rest of the herd.

Between the Civil War and 1912, the United States welcomed twelve new states into the Union. In 1867, Nebraska, settled largely by farmers, achieved statehood. Nine years later, Colorado—still populated almost entirely by miners and those who served them—joined the Union.

The growing network of railroads that linked the nation from coast to coast helped rush the creation of six new states in 1889 and 1890. The railroads had brought farmers to North Dakota. Neighboring South Dakota, after its gold rush, was settled by cattle ranchers. In Montana, miners first occupied the land, followed by cattle ranchers and sheepherders. Cattle ranchers also helped settle the Wyoming Territory. Washington's first permanent settlements were the logging camps and sawmills that served miners in neighboring Idaho.

In 1896, Utah, first settled by Mormons who had applied for statehood almost fifty years earlier, finally joined the Union. In 1907, Oklahoma—which had been reserved by Congress as Indian Territory in 1828—achieved statehood under pressure from white settlers. They had flooded into the region in 1889, when Congress sold 2 million acres of Oklahoma land, despite the 1828 promise to the Indians.

By 1910, as this map indicates, all of the forty-eight continental states except Arizona and New Mexico had achieved statehood. New Mexico was the home of sheep ranchers, cattle ranchers, and farmers all competing for land. In Arizona, ranches and towns had gradually spread over former Indian lands. Both states would join the Union two years later.

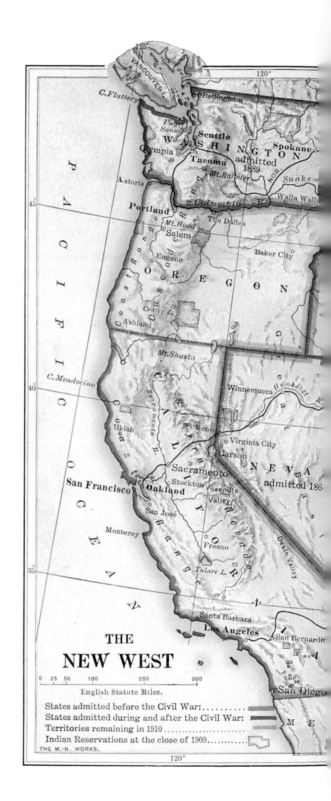

THE
NEW WEST

0 25 50   100   200   300

English Statute Miles.

States admitted before the Civil War:..........
States admitted during and after the Civil War:
Territories remaining in 1910.....................
Indian Reservations at the close of 1909..........
THE M.-N. WORKS.

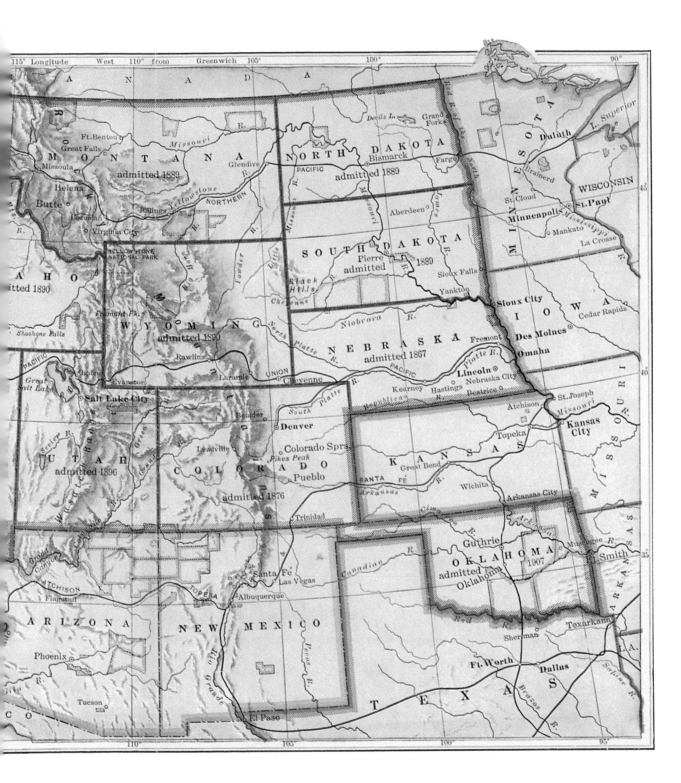

RANCHING IN THE WEST

Cattle ranching in America began with Spanish missionaries in Texas, California, and the Southwest in the middle of the eighteenth century. The Spanish *padres* (priests) trained Native Americans to tend the cattle on their ranches and turned cattle raising into an industry. Missions with thousands of cattle were not at all uncommon. The missions would live on the profits obtained by trading the hides and tallow (rendered fat, used in soap and candles). A cattle-raising culture quickly grew up in California—with many leisure activities, such as roping contests and riding tricks, based on actual work skills.

By the mid-1800s, the ongoing slaughter of the buffalo on the Great Plains left 200,000 square miles of open rangeland that stretched from the Mississippi to the Rockies. This open range soon supported a rapidly growing American cattle industry.

During the 1870s, ranchers, with the help of "cowboys," filled these open plains with millions of cattle, which they drove in herds all the way from Texas. For over thirty years, isolated herds of cattle had been driven from Texas a thousand miles for sale in Missouri markets. But after the Civil War, the drives changed. Cowboys began driving their cattle north to the free grasslands of the Midwestern plains. By feeding them on vast public lands, cattle ranchers could fatten their cattle (and therefore increase their value) at almost no cost. This strategy allowed ranchers to make fortunes on the open range.

Cattle ranchers raised cows, bulls, and steers (bulls that had been castrated). These two animals (right) won prizes as the "Queen of Cattle" (best cow) and the "Champion Steer" at an 1886 fair.

This 1885 illustration (below), originally used as the frontispiece to A Texas Cow Boy, a popular book about cowboy life, depicts many aspects of life in a cow camp. In the right foreground, a cowboy sports fancy gear, while on the left, the camp cook prepares a meal from the back of his chuck wagon. Cowboys in the background ride the herd, while the two cowboys at center work at roping in a stray that has wandered from the herd.

The cattle industry presented work opportunities for those freed slaves who went West following the Civil War. As many as one-third of the cowboys on the cattle trails from Texas to the Midwest were black. This photograph (right) by Erwin E. Smith shows a group of black cowboys posing at a fair in Bonham, Texas.

Most ranchers started out living in tents, one-room shacks, or dugouts cut in hillsides. Those fortunate enough to achieve success on the range could build houses like the one shown on this small spread in the Dakotas (below). Only the most prosperous ranchers could afford plank floors, glass windows, second stories, and side porches.

Indians were actually the first American cowboys. Long before whites had adopted the riding and roping skills that allowed them to subdue wild bulls and control herds of cattle, Native Americans had already perfected these arts. The Native American in this photograph (above), carrying a lariat perhaps 100 feet long, worked as a cowboy on the Montana range.

THE DANGERS OF OPEN-RANGE RANCHING

Open-range ranching posed many dangers for cowboys. Occasionally Native Americans, who regarded the ranchers as trespassers on their land, would conduct a raid on one of the herds. After trying to stampede the cattle, these raiders would make off with as many of the stragglers as they could.

Much more common than Indian raids, however, were attacks by white desperadoes. Cattle rustlers and horse thieves would steal cattle or horses roaming free on the range. As soon as possible, they would try to blur or change the brands (the owners' marks) on the cattle, thereby building herds that they could drive to other markets for sale. Originally working alone, rustlers began organizing into outlaw gangs in order to make more money. By 1883, as much as three percent of the cattle on the open range was being lost to rustlers.

When unoccupied grassland began to be taken up by a flood of newcomers, range wars broke out. Because cattle needed a lot of land for grazing, the demand for land often led to armed struggles to settle the question of who had more right to range on public land. The range wars heated up in the 1880s, when an ever-increasing number of small ranchers began moving onto land already claimed—but not legally owned—by powerful cattle barons or cattle companies. These battles became so heated that they sometimes led to shoot-outs, lynchings, and hangings.

This illustration from an 1874 issue of Harper's Weekly (opposite, top) shows the violence of a cattle raid. Cattle rustlers sometimes engaged in close-range shooting with groups of cowboys trying to protect their herds. Eventually, cowboys began copying the rustlers themselves, organizing into groups to seek revenge. These lynching parties would track down rustlers and hang them from the nearest tree or railroad bridge.

This painting by Frederic Remington (1861–1909; opposite, bottom) shows a weary cowboy heading back to camp after a long night tending the herd. On the open range, herds needed guarding at night—not only against rustlers, who often conducted their raids after dark, but also against any fright that might cause the cattle to stampede.

SHEEP RANCHING

Cattle ranchers were not the only pioneers to establish homes on the open range. Sheepherders also found these free grasslands a cheap way to graze their herds. In Montana alone, the sheep population rose from 4,000 in 1870 to over 4 million by 1900, while in Wyoming the sheep population grew from 6,000 to 5 million in the same period.

For many ranchers, sheep were more profitable than cattle. As the growth of the railroads made it easier to get wool and meat to Eastern markets, sheep ranching quickly became one of the leading industries of the West.

Wild animals and the harsh weather all posed a threat to the sheepherder's flock. But the biggest threat came from the cattle ranchers, who resented the sheepherders moving in on what they considered their territory. They had no legal claim to the land but thought they were entitled to it because they were there first. Also, most cattle ranchers believed large herds of sheep could eat grass down to its roots and then destroy even the roots with their sharp hooves, ruining cattle-grazing land.

The worst range wars were fought between cattle ranchers and sheepherders. Cattle ranchers resorted to desperate measures to drive sheep off the range—including poisoning the grass with saltpeter (toxic to sheep but not to cattle) and sheep raids.

Sheepherding was a solitary job, since one man alone could handle as many as 3,000 sheep—a herd that would produce 20,000 pounds of wool every year. Although some sheepherders went months without seeing other human beings, the herder pictured (right) brought his family with him to the mountains, where sheep could graze in the summer months.

At first, cattle ranchers conducted raids merely to scare both sheepherders and sheep, scatter the flocks, and force the herders to move on. But in their desperation, cattle raiders later used clubs, rifles, dynamite, and fire to destroy the flocks. Sometimes they might drive a herd over a cliff or into a bed of quicksand. This 1867 illustration from Harper's Weekly (below) shows masked riders killing sheep while holding the herders at gunpoint.

LIFE ON THE RANGE

Open-range ranches were revived in Texas after the Civil War. Cut off from Northern markets because of the conflict, cattle ranchers had little reason to continue ranching. They let their herds roam. As a result, the population of wild Texas cattle grew from 3.5 million in 1860 to 6 million in 1865. When the war ended and markets opened up again, Texas longhorns were a rich natural resource. Open-range ranchers would gather a herd of longhorns, fatten them up, and then drive the cattle north to sell in the cattle markets growing up in Kansas and Missouri.

Life on the ranch and range was difficult, dusty, and boring. Many cowboys spent up to eighteen hours a day, seven days a week, tending cattle and doing chores. Their main duty was keeping the cattle healthy and together—a job that included finding good grazing land, dehorning cattle, tracking down strays, pulling cows out of bogs, nursing injured animals, maintaining a constant fire watch in the dry summer months, harvesting hay for the horses, and gathering dried cow manure to use as fuel for fires.

During the winter months, most large ranches laid off more than half their cowboys. Many would roam from ranch to ranch offering to do repair work or chores in return for meals.

Horses were extremely important to the Plains Indians, who depended on them for hunting and moving camp. In this engraving (above) from a painting by Frederic Remington, an Indian and his son work together to "break" a wild pony. Their training method, relying on a strong rope, a tight grip, and determination, was later adapted for horse-training on Western ranches.

Because cows could drink up to thirty gallons of water a day, cowboys on the range needed to know all of the nearest sources of good drinking water. (Water tainted with alkali deposits could kill cattle if they drank too much of it.) The importance of water meant that whoever controlled the water ruled the land. The thirsty cattle pictured here (opposite, top) are cooling themselves in and drinking from the Wichita River.

Every spring, cowboys would try to add to their stock of horses—the most important piece of "equipment" on the ranch—by taming wild four-year-old horses. The broncobuster photographed here (opposite, bottom) has already corralled, roped, and bridled a wild mustang. He still needs to calm the horse before trying to saddle and ride it. This dangerous work, which was painful for the horse, aimed to teach the mustangs to fear and respect the cowboy and to obey him.

Cowboys spent many of their daylight hours on their horses. This bored cowhand (above) from the Bar Diamond Ranch remains on his horse even while lounging. While tending the herd, cowboys needed to stay on their horses even when they had nothing to do—just in case a stampede, fire, or other emergency called for immediate action.

The wagon cook (opposite, top), responsible for keeping the cowboys contented on the range, was the first person up in the morning and often the last to bed down at night. He fixed three hot meals a day, beginning with a predawn breakfast of beans, biscuits, and coffee, often served with bacon or fatty pork. The two main meals of the day, one served at noon after the morning's work and the other after the day's work was done, consisted of stews, bacon, various pies and puddings, and on rare occasions barbecued fresh beef.

The chuck wagon, driven by the cook, carried all of the cowboys' gear, medical supplies, and food. For this reason, it was the center of camp life. The cowboys photographed here (opposite, bottom), employed by the Matador Land and Cattle Company, gather under tents for dinner after a long day's work at the Turtle Hole Division roundup camp.

ON THE TRAIL

Cattle drives that pushed herds along trails for hundreds or even thousands of miles allowed ranchers to expand their trade enormously. Rather than waiting for the market to come to them, ranchers drove the cattle to wherever the demand was greatest.

The practice began on a small scale as early as the 1830s, when Texas cattle were driven to Louisiana. The 1840s and 1850s also saw some big cattle drives from Kansas to the Oregon Territory, and from Texas to California in the wake of the Gold Rush. Yet the practice of driving cattle to markets did not become common on a large scale until after the Civil War.

The increasing Texas cattle population had driven the local price of Texas longhorns down. Yet elsewhere the price of cattle remained as much as ten times higher than in Texas. The possibility for enormous profits convinced ranchers and cowboys to brave the Plains with enormous herds of cattle. They faced the dangers of Indian raids, grass fires, stampedes, and the armed opposition of Kansas and Missouri livestock farmers, who set up guards to prevent Texas longhorns (which they thought carried disease) from infecting their cattle.

Despite the risks, ranchers drove 4 million cattle out of Texas between 1869 and 1881. In 1870, the peak year, 600,000 longhorns made their way north along the trail.

Cowboys would drive their herds to cow towns like Dodge City and Abilene at the end of the trail. This engraving, first published in Frank Leslie's Illustrated Newspaper *in 1878 (right), shows what it looked like when cowboys led their thundering herds down one of the main streets of Dodge City, Kansas. Here, the herds would be sold and shipped East by rail, or trailed farther north to stock the ranges of Kansas, Nebraska, the Dakotas, and Montana.*

Life on the trail consisted of two months or more of boring, dusty days. Around a dozen cowboys would surround and guide a herd of two or three thousand head. Traveling only ten to fifteen miles a day, the cowboys and their herd would travel 650 miles or more to reach their markets. This 1904 painting by Frederic Remington (below) portrays a cowboy leading a herd of longhorns along the trail.

CATTLE RAISING AS BIG BUSINESS

The focus of the cattle business changed from hides and tallow to beef in the late 1860s and the 1870s. Because of the high demand for beef in the East, the cattle business boomed in the 1870s, and even more so in the 1880s. By the middle of the 1880s, the beef cattle industry had become by far the biggest business in the West.

The beef bonanza helped build several boomtowns, most of them in Kansas—Abilene, Dodge City, Wichita, and Ellsworth. All were located along railroad lines because the railroads played such an important role in the growth of the cattle business. The railroads allowed the cattle to reach the hungry markets of the East quickly.

Cattle agents would descend on the Kansas boomtowns, competing to buy the cattle driven up from Texas or down from Montana and the Dakotas. The agents would then ship the live cattle to marketplaces in the East, and sell them to meat-packing houses at a handsome profit.

In 1875, the meat-packing houses began moving west—at least as far as Chicago, a central connection for all the railroads running through Kansas and Nebraska. The invention of refrigerated rail cars allowed enterprising meat packers like Gustavus Swift (1839–1903) and Philip D. Armour (1832–1901) to make fortunes. By opening slaughterhouses in Chicago, they no longer had to ship whole animals by rail; now they could ship only the meat East—or even back West, where both cities and the market for beef were growing.

Illustrated souvenir maps, like this one promoting Wichita, Kansas (opposite, top), attempted to attract settlers to the new cities of the West. Statistics highlight Wichita's rapidly growing population, high property values, railroad routes, building construction, and real estate sales.

Once cattle were slaughtered in the stockyards, their carcasses were butchered and kept in cold storage. From there they were shipped in refrigerated rail cars to meat markets. This woodcut (opposite, bottom) shows a bustling meat market on the West Coast, where wild game is being sold alongside beef.

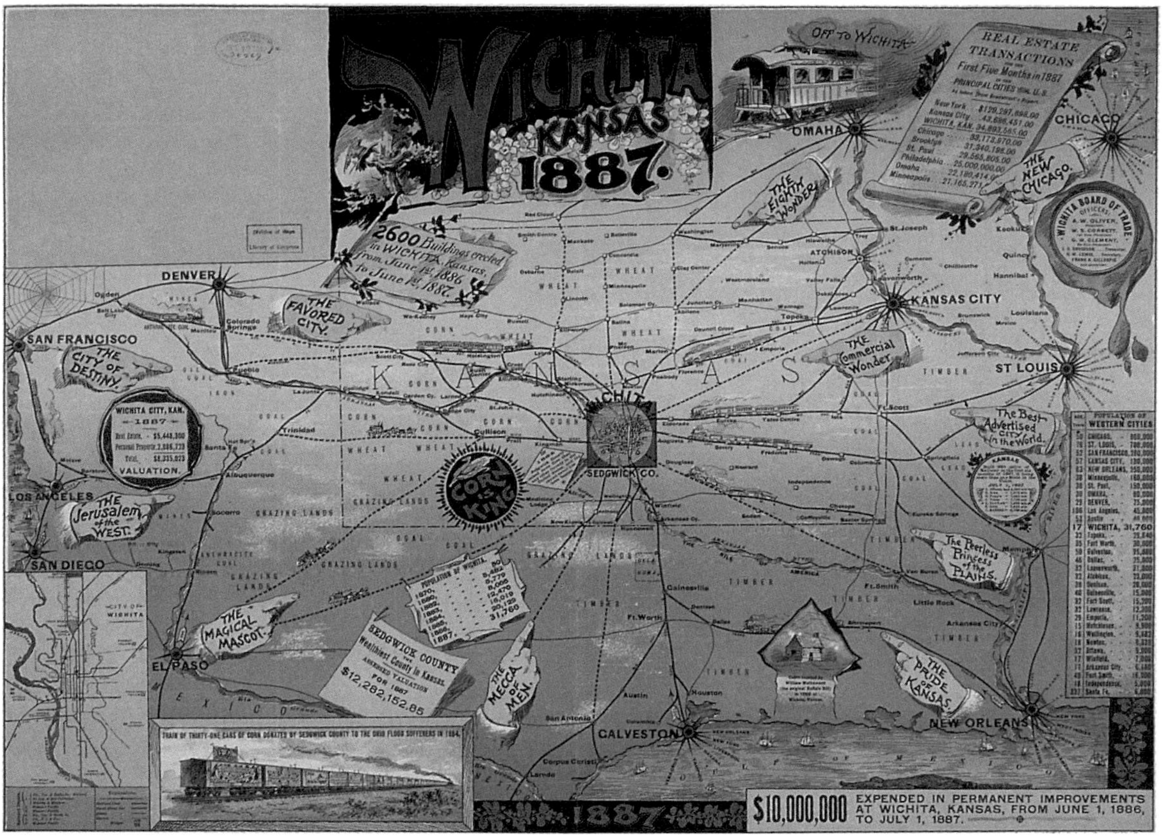
WICHITA KANSAS 1887.
OFF TO WICHITA
REAL ESTATE TRANSACTIONS
First Five Months in 1887
PRINCIPAL CITIES
OMAHA
CHICAGO
THE NEW CHICAGO.
THE EIGHTH WONDER
WICHITA BOARD OF TRADE
2600 Buildings erected in WICHITA, Kansas, from June 1st 1886 to June 1st 1887.
DENVER
THE FAVORED CITY.
SAN FRANCISCO
THE CITY of DESTINY
KANSAS CITY
ATCHISON
THE Commercial Wonder
ST LOUIS
K A N S A S
WHEAT
CORN
WICHITA
SEDGWICK CO.
CORN IS KING
WICHITA CITY, KAN. 1887
VALUATION.
LOS ANGELES
THE Jerusalem of the WEST.
SAN DIEGO
The Best Advertised CITY in the World.
POPULATION OF WESTERN CITIES
The Peerless Princess of the PLAINS.
POPULATION OF WICHITA.
GRAZING LANDS
TIMBER
CITY OF WICHITA
THE MAGICAL MASCOT.
SEDGWICK COUNTY Wealthiest County in Kansas. ASSESSED VALUATION FOR 1887 $12,282,152.85
THE MECCA OF MEX.
THE PRIDE OF KANSAS
EL PASO
GALVESTON
NEW ORLEANS
TRAIN OF THIRTY-ONE CARS OF CORN DONATED BY SEDGWICK COUNTY TO THE OHIO FLOOD SUFFERERS IN 1884.
1887
$10,000,000 EXPENDED IN PERMANENT IMPROVEMENTS AT WICHITA, KANSAS, FROM JUNE 1, 1886, TO JULY 1, 1887.

MARKET
NEW WORLD MARKET
EAGLE

END OF THE TRAIL

At the end of a cattle drive, cowboys would usually get paid in full as soon as the herd was sold. This gave them a lot of money to spend, and no place to spend it but the cow town itself.

The cow town offered many cowboys their only chance both to carouse and to find some human companionship. But first they had to make themselves presentable. After months on the trail with no change of clothes, the dust-covered cowboys would usually head for a boardinghouse to bathe before doing anything else. They might also visit the barber for a shave and a haircut, and one of the haberdashers to splurge on some fancy clothes.

Many cowboys would celebrate the end of the trail and the money in their pockets with a night of revelry. The place for much of this activity—drinking, poker playing, dancing with barmaids, striking deals for the next year's cattle drive, and getting into brawls—was one of the local saloons. And saloons weren't in short supply. In most cow towns, saloons outnumbered all other business establishments combined.

Although some permanent settlers were not pleased by this flood of hard-drinking rowdies, the merchants and other business owners who benefited from the cowboys' free spending ways took a more tolerant view. And they had good reason: In the end, the cow town itself ate up most of the cowboys' wages.

On the ranch, where not enough women were available to dance, some cowboys would usually be designated to dance the female parts. So when cowboys arrived in a cow town at the end of the trail, one of the first things many of them wanted to do was get cleaned up and head for a fandango like the fellows in this engraving are doing (opposite, top)—a lavish dance with real women.

After dropping off their herds at the stock-yards—usually located near the railroad station—the cowboys would start to cel-ebrate. The cowboys pictured here (oppo-site, bottom) have all stopped in a nearby rail yard to have a swig of liquor.

FARMING

In the eighteenth century, colonial American farmers moved toward commercial agriculture. By 1750, most of the settled land was devoted to growing crops such as rice, wheat, and tobacco for export to Europe.

When the frontier moved west of the Appalachian Mountains after the French and Indian War (1754–63), pioneering farmers began cultivating grains and livestock east of the Mississippi River and west of the Appalachian Mountains. Many of the farmers in the early nineteenth century would find a plot of government land, clear it of trees, build a house and a farm, and gain "ownership." "Squatting" on public land, which plains ranchers would do fifty years later, was legalized by the Preemption Act of 1830, which allowed squatters to purchase the land they had settled from the government.

The 1862 Homestead Act, which offered 160 acres of free land to any adult male who established five years' residence on it, aimed to expand American presence in the West by luring farmers onto the prairies. Yet most farmers in the East wondered whether the land was worth the effort. Most viewed the prairie as a desolate wasteland.

The pioneering cattle ranchers, however, tending small vegetable gardens and cultivating hay to feed their horses, showed that crops would in fact grow on the plains. And the rapidly expanding railway network made it much easier for farmers to transport these crops. These developments convinced homesteaders to take the risk. The land rush was on.

Until the eighteenth century, farmers sowed their crops by scattering seeds after plowing their fields. A more efficient and economical planting method became possible when British farmer Jethro Tull (1674–1741) invented the horse-drawn seed drill, which would drill small holes in the ground and automatically drop seeds into these fresh holes. The invention encouraged many imitations and improved machinery, like Cooke's patent drill machine, pictured here (right).

Until the Civil War, Southern plantations— large estates that depended largely on slave labor to plant and harvest crops—were a model for agriculture in America. As pioneering farmers pushed west of the Alleghenies, they attempted to copy the commercial success of these plantations by establishing their own frontier plantations, like the one shown in this 1768 engraving from Scenographic Americana *(below).*

HOMESTEADERS

From the late 1870s through the 1880s, an enormous wave of newcomers arrived in the West to establish permanent settlements. They included native-born Americans of English descent and recent immigrants from Germany, Norway, Sweden, and Russia. At first these homesteaders moved just west of the Mississippi. Later they pushed farther into the West, crossing the Plains all the way to the Rockies.

Many of these homesteaders, also known as sodbusters or grangers, took advantage of the trails blazed and the towns built earlier by ranchers and miners. The growth of railroads allowed more homesteaders to arrive in the West by train rather than in wagons. Some clustered around established cow towns. Others planted farms around mining towns—at first just to meet miners' needs but later producing a surplus of cash crops. As the railroads carried the crops away for sale, the homesteaders' success drew more and more settlers westward.

By 1900, most Americans—not only in the West, but all the way across the country—lived or worked on farms, or were otherwise economically dependent on the farmers. Village stores met the farmers' needs, as did traveling merchants who brought retail goods directly to the consumers. Churches and lodges for farmers, known as Grange halls, were the center of social activity. But daily life, from before dawn to sunset, consisted largely of completing the many chores involved in operating a farm.

This illustration, published in one of the many state and county "atlases" that appeared in the 1870s and 1880s, shows a successful homestead ranch in Kansas. On a typical day, the farmer and his hired hands might need to plow the fields, cultivate the vegetable crops and fruit trees, work with the horses, and tend the penned livestock.

FARMING IN THE WEST

One of the biggest obstacles to pioneer farmers as the frontier moved farther westward across the Great Plains was the lack of trees. Although earlier pioneers had found clearing the forests a backbreaking chore, this new generation of pioneer farmers recognized wood as a much-needed source of fuel, as well as a material for construction of houses, furniture, and other necessities.

Plains farmers also had to overcome a lack of water. Throughout the 1880s, windmills began to appear across the plains, providing a solution to the problem by using wind power to pump water from freshly dug wells.

The weather on the prairie was a major hardship as well. One year— 1887—was especially difficult, beginning with a devastating blizzard and continuing with a scorching summer drought. The crushing combination, and its effect on their crops and livestock, drove many homesteaders from the plains.

Despite these hardships, crops could and did grow on the plains. And the plains offered endless stretches of free and fertile land, easily plowed without clearing the land of trees. The ever-expanding railroad network crisscrossing the West made it easy and inexpensive to transport crops to large markets. With these incentives, hundreds of thousands of homesteaders began cultivating corn and wheat, the most profitable crop of the plains.

Farms in the West were self-sufficient because they were usually located far away from cities and towns. Families made their own clothes and provisions rather than purchasing these goods from stores. This engraving (right), from a painting by Frederic Remington, shows a woman from the Southwest making tortillas, using flour ground from Indian corn.

Farmers found the prairie to be an excellent environment for growing wheat. This engraving of a prairie farm is the frontispiece to a book written in 1869 by Alfred R. Waud, entitled Where to Emigrate and Why, *which was a useful guide to farmers interested in moving to the West.*

RAISING LIVESTOCK ON FARMS

Although the invention of complex machines made farming the West easier, one simple innovation truly transformed the West: the invention of barbed wire in 1874. Homesteading farmers with 160 acres of land needed to protect their crops from the cattle and other animals ranging across the open plains. The increasingly crowded cattle ranchers also wanted some way of marking off their grazing lands and keeping their herds separate. With wood scarce, the invention of barbed wire provided a cheap and easily-erected kind of fencing.

The introduction of barbed wire meant the beginning of the end of open-range ranching—although the business managed to survive until ferocious blizzards in the winter of 1886–87 killed hundreds of thousands of open-range cattle. Where they once squatted on the open range, ranchers began to acquire land legally, fencing it with barbed wire, digging wells, erecting windmills and pumps, irrigating the fields, and raising fodder crops. Livestock farms—stocked chiefly with cattle, sheep, and pigs—began popping up throughout the West. Unlike the open-range ranches, livestock farms sheltered their animals during the bitterly cold winter months, feeding them stored fodder when snow covered the grazing lands. By 1900, the great livestock ranches had been established in the West.

This 1885 lithograph (below), titled "Butcher's Delight," shows a prosperous livestock farm in the late nineteenth century. Although the livestock continued to graze in open fields, these grazing grounds were now legally owned by the rancher. Even the longhorn cattle no longer ran wild.

INVENTIONS AND TECHNOLOGY

The expansion of the railroads created an enormous market for the grain and meat of the West. This increased demand encouraged farmers to invent new machinery and improved techniques to plow, plant, and harvest their crops.

The mechanization of the farm began with the introduction of the seed drill, marketed on a wide scale in the 1830s. In 1836, blacksmith and plowmaker John Deere (1804–86) invented a tool that proved indispensable to farmers on the prairie: the steel plow. The rich black soil of the prairie tended to clog standard iron plows. The steel plow let farmers till the soil of the prairie, and also needed less animal power to turn the soil. The horse-drawn cultivator also became popular in the 1860s and 1870s.

Invented in 1831, the reaper, a machine that cuts grain, found its market when farmers began moving onto the prairie. The first harvester, which not only cut grain but then swept it onto a conveyor that carried it to a box for binding, was patented in 1858.

Threshers, which separate wheat and other grains from the straw and chaff, also became mechanized in the nineteenth century. Horse-drawn models, first introduced in 1837, gave way to large stationary threshers powered by steam engines, which came into use near the end of the century. And in the late 1880s, a combine harvester—a machine that both cuts and threshes grains—was introduced in California.

Cyrus Hall McCormick (1809–84) developed the mechanical reaper in 1831, which allowed farmers to harvest their crops without hiring lots of expensive farmhands. Thirteen years later, McCormick had sold less than one hundred reapers. He opened a Chicago factory in 1847 that he hoped would meet the needs of the barely settled prairie states of the Midwest. Within ten years, McCormick was selling over 4,000 reapers a year. By 1883, when this advertisement was first published, the words "McCormick" and "reaper" were inseparable.

Horse-drawn cultivators, like the one seen in this 1866 advertisement, were developed in the mid-nineteenth century. The shovels, or blades, straddle the rows of crops, dislodging the soil around them to uproot and destroy weeds that might choke the plants. The farmer in this illustration could cultivate fifteen acres a day using this machine.

Before beginning to plow the ground, farmers needed to clear the grasslands that had earlier fed so many grazing cattle and sheep. This advertising trade card for the Climax Mower, manufactured by the Corry Machine Company of Corry, Pennsylvania, first appeared in the 1880s.

The Grange, officially known as the Patrons of Husbandry, was founded in 1867. Farmers came to use the organization to achieve political ends, including fair railroad rates, land grants, and other agricultural policies favorable to farmers. The Grange reached its heyday in the mid-1870s, when almost every state had at least one local unit and nationwide membership approached 800,000. This poster (above), called "Gift for the Grangers," shows various farm scenes as well as social gatherings and political meetings sponsored by the Grange.

When Oliver H. Kelley (1826–1913) founded the Patrons of Husbandry in 1867, he conceived of it not as a political organization but as an educational and social one. Kelley hoped that the organization would advance the cause of farmers by instructing them in valuable agricultural practices. Students who excelled in agricultural courses received certificates like the one pictured here (below, top).

In most farming and ranching communities, the biggest event of the year was the county fair. This 1888 Currier & Ives lithograph, "Sights of the Fairgrounds" (below, bottom), shows a typical county fair of the late nineteenth century. Various contests judged horses' grooming, jumping, and speed on the racetrack. Owners of cattle, sheep, and pigs would compete for ribbons awarded for size, fullness of coat, and other physical attributes.

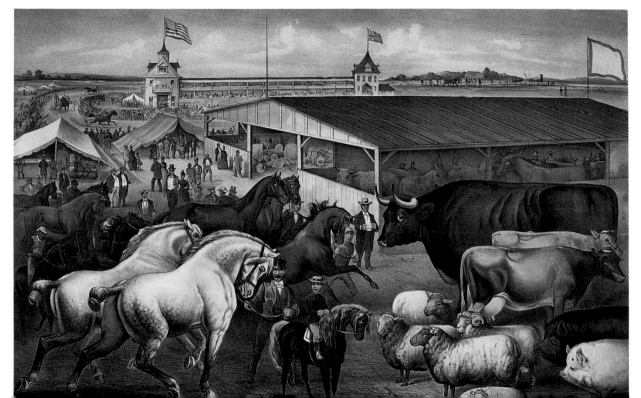

BLACK GOLD

As settlement expanded westward, many homesteads found themselves well beyond the range of city gas supplies. The need for local sources of crude oil to manufacture kerosene increased dramatically. Kerosene for oil lamps—and later for use in kerosene-burning engines—was the principal product manufactured from crude oil in the second half of the nineteenth century. (Gasoline was considered a waste product until the twentieth century, when it became the chief fuel for automobiles.) In the wake of the Industrial Revolution, oil was needed not just as a source of illumination and as a lubricant, but as a source of energy, especially for industry. The growing demand for petroleum products led to a boom in the exploration and drilling of oil wells all over the country.

The oil industry was still young in the second half of the nineteenth century. Edwin L. Drake (1819–80) had drilled through sixty-nine feet of rock in Titusville, Pennsylvania, to complete the first oil well in the world in August 1859. The industry grew quickly. By the end of the century, drilling for oil had swept through the United States—especially through the West. In 1901, the Spindletop gusher outside of Beaumont, Texas—the first major oil field in the state—forever transformed the economy of the region. By that time, however, oil fields had already been discovered in fourteen states, including Oklahoma, Colorado, Wyoming, and California.

Oil was discovered in Texas on January 10, 1901, when a black geyser of oil shot 200 feet into the air from Spindletop Mound. This photograph (above) shows an oilfield in Saratoga, Texas, in 1908.

Just as the discovery of gold had created mining boomtowns, and the laying down of railroad tracks had generated cattle boomtowns, the discovery of oil—and the work and fortunes it promised—led to the formation of oil boomtowns. This illustration from Harper's Weekly (right), entitled "Saturday Noon," portrays a street scene in an Oklahoma oil boomtown in the late nineteenth century.

Resource Guide

Key to picture positions: (T) top, (C) center, (B) bottom; and in combinations: (TL) top left, (TC) top center, (TR) top right, (BL) bottom left, (BC) bottom center, (BR) bottom right.

Key to picture locations within the Library of Congress collections (and where available, photo negative numbers): P - Prints and Photographs;

HABS - Historical American Buildings Survey (div. of Prints and Photographs); R - Rare Book Division; G - General Collections; MSS - Manuscript Division; G&M - Geography and Map Division.

PICTURES IN THIS VOLUME

2-3 Cowboys, P 4-5 Miner, P 6-7 Cabin, P

Timeline: 8-9 TL,Washington, P; BL, Cook, P, USZ62-102228; TR, mansion, P, USZ62-20528; BR, map, MSS 10-11 TL, Monroe, G; TR, masthead, MSS; BR, Independence, P, USZ62-3667 12-13 TL, Stowe, P; BL, land office, P, USZ62-65462; TR, Lincoln, P; BR, mine, P, USZ62-1320 14-15 TL, Chinese, P; TR, DuBois, G; BR, raid, P, USZ62-55596

Part I: 16-17 Log, P 18-19 C, map, G 20-21 TR, map, R; BR, trading, P, USZ62-45595 22-23 TR, Crockett, R; BR, cabin, R 24-25 TL, Indian attack, R; BR, bear, P 26-27 TL, beaver, G; BC, boat, P, USZ62-735 28-29 C, fox, P 30-31 BC, fort, P, USZ62-7283; TR, mountain man, P, USZ62-53324 32-33 C, buffalo, P 34-35 BL, hunt, P; TR, fire, P 36-37 TC, train, P, USZ62-44084; BR, title page, P, USZ62-55602 38-39 TR, skulls, G; BR, drinking, P, USZ62-37832 40-41 C, bear, P, USZ62-8114 42-43 BC, camp, P, USZ62-5347; TR, mining, P 44-45 TL, panning, P, USZ62-7120; BL, mill, P, USZ62-48138; TR, process, P 46-47 TL, mining, P; TR, Virginia City, P, USZ62-7743; BR, map, G&M 48-49 TL, woman, P, USZ62-8894; TR,

Leadville, P, USZ62-1482; BL, gulch, P 50-51 BC, Denver, R; TR, San Francisco, P 52-53 BL, tree, P; TR, logging, P 54-55 TL, wagon, P, USZ62-56645; TR, circle, P, USZ62-63586

Part II: 56-57 Cowboy, R 58-59 Map, G 60-61 BC, camp, P; TR, cattle, P 62-63 TL, Indian cowboy, P, USZ62-055136; TR, black cowboys, P; BR, ranch, P, USZ62-22250 64-65 TR, cattle, P, USZ62-055596; BR, cowboy, R 66-67 BC, sheep raid, P, USZ62-8477; TR, house, P 68-69 TL, Indians, G; TR, watering hole, P, USZ62-5591; BR, bronco, P, USZ62-917 70-71 TL, horse, P, USZ62-559563; TR, chuck wagon, P, USZ62-55990; BR, eating, P, USZ62-559430 72-73 BC, cattle, P; TR, town, P, USZ62-7792 74-75 TR, map, R; BR, maret, P 76-77 TR, fandango, P, USZ62-00862; BR, train,P 78-79 BC, farm, P, USZ62-31185; TR, drill, P, USZ62-55537 80-81 C, homesteaders, P 82-83 T, woman, G; B, home, P, USZ62-676 84-85 C, cows, R 86-87 C, reaper, R 88-89 BL, cultivator, G; TR, mower, P, USZ62-14084 90-91 TL, granger, P, USZ62-1048; TR, reward, P, USZ-40911; BR, fair, P 92-93 TL, oil well, P; TR, town, P, USZ62-876

SUGGESTED READING

AMERICAN HERITAGE. *The California Gold Rush.* Mahwah, New Jersey: Troll Associates, 1961.
—*Cowboys and Cattle Country.* Mahwah, New Jersey: Troll Associates, 1961.
—*Trappers and Mountain Men.* Mahwah, New Jersey: Troll Associates, 1961.
DANIEL, CLIFTON. *Chronicle of America.* New York: Prentice Hall, 1989.
JOSEPHY, ALVIN. *The World Almanac of the American West.* New York: Pharos Books, 1986.

MORRISON, SAMUEL. *The Oxford History of the American People.* New York: Oxford University Press, 1965.
TIME-LIFE. *The Ranchers.* Alexandria, Virginia: Time-Life Books, 1977.
—*The Cowboys.* Alexandria, Virginia: Time-Life Books, 1976.
—*The Miners.* Alexandria, Virginia: Time-Life Books, 1973.

Index